MW00787206

ADOLESCENT LITERACY SERIES

Figurative Language

Susan Brooks-Young

SGS-SFI/COC-US09/5501

1   2   3   4   5   6   7   8   9   10

ISBN 978-0-8251-6286-2

Copyright © 2008

J. Weston Walch, Publisher

40 Walch Drive • Portland, ME 04103

www.walch.com

Printed in the United States of America

Table of Contents

Introduction

Effective instruction in adolescent literacy does not rely on one strategy alone. Reading, writing, listening and speaking all contribute to vocabulary acquisition. The subtleties of vocabulary development do, however, lend themselves to both direct and indirect instruction. Most struggling readers can, and do, read printed words. Their difficulty is not in articulating, or even spelling, the printed text. The challenge to this learner is an inability to understand, process, and communicate the ideas expressed by the words.

The nature of this problem in adolescent literacy reaches deeper than a student's comprehension. The inability to comprehend text impacts a learner's ability to actively learn new words. The result is that a student will struggle to understand, learn, and communicate concepts in all subject areas. This is our call to action. This is the rationale for providing teachers like you with the resources you need to not only provide students with direct, explicit vocabulary instruction, but to provide you with the materials for students to transfer strategies to the content areas.

This title focuses on helping students to develop their ability to understand, analyze, and apply figurative language. Figurative language is the use of a non-literal statement to symbolize meaning that enhances an idea. It has been cited in many studies as serving a role in reading comprehension, fluency, language abilities, and life experience. For learners, skillfulness in understanding and using figurative language enriches academic and social development. Specifically, figurative language is important for increasing oral communication, reading comprehension, effective writing, and vocabulary acquisition.

The 20 lessons set forth in this book will provide students with models for instruction and application of figurative language in a variety of contexts organized around reading, vocabulary, and writing. Used to extend and enhance your existing curriculum, each lesson is intended to target instruction of a specific figure of speech. Activities and instruction range from 20 to 50 minutes to complete.

Said What?

Class Configuration

Time required:

one class period (approximately 45–50 minutes)

Structure:

pair (activity sheet), group (class discussion)

Materials:

- 1 copy of each activity sheet for each student
- reference books about origins of idioms such as *Scholastic Dictionary of Idioms* (Revised) by Marvin Terban or *The Oxford Dictionary of Idioms* (Oxford Paperback Reference) by Judith Siefring
- If you have access to the Internet, you may also want to use web sites such as Meanings and Origins of Phrases, Sayings, and Idioms (www.phrases.org.uk/meanings/index.html) or IdiomSite.com (www.idiomsite.com).

Learning objectives:

- Students will contribute at least one entry to an idiom "book." Each entry includes the origin of the idiom, the current meaning, and a sentence using the idiom.

Standards

IRA/NCTE

3. Students apply a wide range of strategies to comprehend, interpret, evaluate, and appreciate texts. They draw on their prior experience, their interactions with other readers and writers, their knowledge of word meaning and of other texts, their word identification strategies, and their understanding of textual features (e.g., sound-letter correspondence, sentence structure, context, graphics).

McREL

Language Arts: Standard 5. Uses the general skills and strategies of the reading process

Said What?

Laying the Groundwork

Accessing students' prior knowledge will help them to develop new skills. Before starting this lesson, make sure students understand concepts such as the following:

- Idioms are expressions that do not literally mean what they say.

- Idioms are used frequently in written and oral language and must be understood to comprehend what is being read or heard.

- Idioms are one of the biggest challenges when learning to speak a new language.

Students should be familiar with the following vocabulary:

idiom   an expression in any language which has a meaning that cannot be figured out using a literal translation.

Teaching Tip

Review the list of twenty idioms on the student page. You may want to add or delete idioms before having students complete the activity. For example, it might be appropriate to include idioms from a novel or short story being read as an assignment.

Decide ahead of time how you will assign idioms to each pair of students, and if you will assign more than one idiom to each pair. If you want pairs to work on more than one idiom, you will need to add more idioms to the list before the lesson or during the group discussion.

Instructional Guide/Procedure

- Ask students to pair up.

- Distribute the activity sheets.

- Ask students to review the list of idioms and brainstorm additional idioms that can be added to the list.

- As students are completing the idiom entries remind them to do the following:

  - Rephrase the information about the origin of the idiom so it will make sense to an English language learner.

  - Double-check the current meaning for accuracy.

  - Use a sentence that clearly demonstrates the meaning of the idiom.

Said What?

Supporting All Learners

- Students who are struggling with writing the idiom entry will benefit from working with a partner. If they need additional time, allow these students to complete the entry as homework.

- Support English language learners by making sure they clearly understand the meaning of the idiom they are assigned. It may be helpful to ask them to illustrate the literal meaning of the idiom. If they need additional time, allow these students to complete the entry as homework.

- Challenge students who are ready for more by asking them to design the format for the idiom book.

Assessment

There are various ways to assess student understanding beyond their completion of the activity sheet. Choose one or more of the following methods to evaluate their learning:

- Ask each student to add at least one additional idiom entry to the book.

- Have student pairs write a sample conversation for their idiom entry.

- Ask students to write a reflection about why idioms can cause confusion in comprehension of written and oral language.

Name _____   Date _____

Said What?

List of Idioms

A bird in the hand is worth two in the bush

A drop in the bucket

A little bird told me

Back to the drawing board

Born with a silver spoon in one's mouth

Caught red handed

Chip on his shoulder

Eat humble pie

Filthy rich

Green-eyed monster

High and dry

In a pickle

In the pink

Learn the ropes

Let the cat out of the bag

Left in the lurch

Not worth a plugged nickel

Once in a blue moon

Red letter day

Wild goose chase

Use the space below to list additional idioms mentioned during the class discussion.

(continued)

Name   Date

Said What?

An **idiom** is an expression in any language which has a meaning that cannot be figured out using a literal translation. For example, a person who is "all thumbs" is clumsy, not disfigured. Idioms are especially confusing for second language learners. However, even a native speaker who understands the meaning of an idiom may not know the origin of the expression.

This activity presents an opportunity for you to provide a service to other students at your school, and to learn about the origins of idioms you hear and/or use every day. Use the form below to work with your partner and write at least one entry for an idiom booklet that will be given to English language learners at your school. Your teacher will assign at least one idiom for you to work on.

Here are two sample entries.

Idiom	Don't throw the baby out with the bath water.
Origin	Several hundred years ago, family members would take turns bathing in a tub of water. The men bathed first, then the women. By the time the children bathed, the water was so dirty that people said it was possible to not see the last baby bathed and throw it out when the tub was emptied.
Current Meaning	Take care. When eliminating the bad parts of something, don't accidentally throw the good out with it.
Sample Sentence	As you consider your decision about closing the park, remember the positive programs that are offered there and don't throw the baby out with the bath water.

Idiom	Get the sack
Origin	This idiom probably refers to tradesmen once owning their own tools, and when they were dismissed from a job would put the tools in a sack and take them away.
Current Meaning	Be fired from a job
Sample Sentence	Robert didn't quit his job; he got the sack.

(continued)

www.walch.com

Name   Date

Said What?

Now work with your partner to complete the chart below.

Idiom	
Origin	
Current Meaning	
Sample Sentence	

Playful Like a Snake? Nonsense Similes

Class Configuration

Time required:

20 minutes

Structure:

individual

Materials:

- 1 copy of the activity sheet for each student

Learning objectives:

- Students will rewrite nonsense similes so that they make sense.

Standards

IRA/NCTE

3. Students apply a wide range of strategies to comprehend, interpret, evaluate, and appreciate texts. They draw on their prior experience, their interactions with other readers and writers, their knowledge of word meaning and of other texts, their word identification strategies, and their understanding of textual features (e.g., sound-letter correspondence, sentence structure, context, graphics).

McREL

Language Arts: Standard 5. Uses the general skills and strategies of the reading process

Laying the Groundwork

Accessing students' prior knowledge will help them to develop new skills. Before starting this lesson, make sure students understand concepts such as the following:

- Authors use similes to make their writing more interesting.

- For similes to enhance writing, they need to make sense.

Students should be familiar with the following vocabulary:

simile   a figure of speech that compares two unlike things using the words *like* or *as*

Playful Like a Snake? Nonsense Similes

Teaching Tip

Once the activity is complete, you can extend or enhance the lesson by asking students to identify similes in literature they are reading in class.

Instructional Guide/Procedure

- Distribute the activity sheets.

- Review the directions and give students 10 minutes to complete the activity.

- Ask students to exchange papers and read another student's revisions for each simile. Ask them to mark each revision with an equal sign if it is the same as the one they wrote, or with a plus sign if it is different.

- As students are rewriting the similes remind them to do the following:

  - Think about who or what is being described by the simile.

  - Think about why the comparisons on the activity sheet do not make sense in their current format.

  - Think about multiple ways the simile can be rewritten to make sense.

Supporting All Learners

- Students who are struggling with rewriting the similes will benefit from working with a partner.

- Support English language learners by working through this activity with them as a group.

- Challenge students who are ready for more by asking them to write their own nonsense similes.

Assessment

There are various ways to assess student understanding beyond their completion of the activity sheet. Choose one or more of the following methods to evaluate their learning:

- Conduct observations while students are working.

- Ask students to rewrite each nonsense simile a second time.

- Ask students to write a brief reflection about the similarities and differences between the way they rewrote the similes and the way the similes were rewritten by the students whose papers they reviewed at the end of the activity.

Playful Like a Snake? Nonsense Similes

Answer Key

Answers will vary, but may include the following responses:

1. Carla is as dull as a butter knife.
    Carla is as sharp as a tack.

2. The house was lit up like a lantern.
    The house was dark like a cave.

3. That car is as fast as a jagua.
    That car is as slow as a snail.

4. The child's cheeks were pale like snow.
    The child's cheeks were red like a rose.

5. The wall is as thin as a tissue.
    The wall is as thick as a brick.

6. Alison runs like a rabbit.
    Alison sings like a bird.

7. Ben is as fierce as a lion.
    Ben is as gentle as a lamb.

8. Ramon is weak like a baby.
    Ramon is strong like an ox.

9. Her hands were as warm as toast.
    Her hands were as cold as ice.

10. The puppy grew like a weed.
    The puppy barked like a seal.

Name _____   Date _____

Playful Like a Snake? Nonsense Similes

A **simile** is a figure of speech that compares two unlike things using the words *like* or *as*.

Examples: He is as skinny as a rail.

Her eyes burned like fire.

When two like things are compared, even if *like* or *as* are used, the comparison is not a simile.

Examples: She is as smart as I am.

Your cell phone is like mine.

Even though similes compare two unlike things, the comparison needs to make sense. In the sample similes, it makes sense to say that someone is as skinny as a rail because a rail is thin. It would not make sense to say that a person was as fat as a rail because rails are not fat.

Read the nonsense similes below. Rewrite each simile so it makes sense. (There are at least two ways each nonsense simile can be rewritten.)

1. Carla is as dull as a tack.

2. The house was lit up like a cave.

3. That car is as fast as a snail.

(continued)

Name   Date
_____   _____

Playful Like a Snake? Nonsense Similes

4. The child's cheeks were pale like a rose.

5. The wall is as thin as a brick.

6. Alison runs like a bird.

7. Ben is as gentle as a lion.

8. Ramon is weak like an ox.

9. Her hands were as warm as ice.

10. The puppy grew like a seal.

Hyperbole and Understatement

Class Configuration

Time required:

25 minutes

Structure:

individual (activity sheet), group (discussion)

Materials:

- 1 copy of the activity sheet for each student

Learning objectives:

- Students will write examples of hyperbole and understatement for five different situations.

Standards

IRA/NCTE

3. Students apply a wide range of strategies to comprehend, interpret, evaluate, and appreciate texts. They draw on their prior experience, their interactions with other readers and writers, their knowledge of word meaning and of other texts, their word identification strategies, and their understanding of textual features (e.g., sound-letter correspondence, sentence structure, context, graphics).

McREL

Language Arts: Standard 5. Uses the general skills and strategies of the reading process

Laying the Groundwork

Accessing students' prior knowledge will help them to develop new skills. Before starting this lesson, make sure students understand concepts such as the following:

- One of the most commonly used writing devices is hyperbole, but it can be overdone. Understatement, the opposite of hyperbole is used less often, but can be just as effective in making a point.

Students should be familiar with the following vocabulary:

hyperbole	a deliberate exaggeration that is meant to emphasize a point or to be funny
understatement	a figure of speech that says less than is intended

Adolescent Literacy: Figurative Language

Hyperbole and Understatement

Teaching Tip

Once the activity is completed, you can extend or enhance the lesson by asking students to identify examples of hyperbole and understatement in literature they are reading in class.

Instructional Guide/Procedure

- Distribute the activity sheets.

- Review the directions and give students 10 minutes to complete the activity.

- Ask students to exchange papers and read another student's examples of hyperbole and understatement. Ask them to choose one example to share during a class discussion.

- Lead a brief discussion about the examples students wrote and read.

- As students are writing the examples of hyperbole and understatement, remind them to do the following:

  - Think about critical attributes of each situation that can be used as the basis for hyperbole or understatement.

  - Think about which situations will work best for humor and which will work best for making a point through exaggeration.

  - Consider more than one way to write each statement.

Supporting All Learners

- Students who are struggling with writing the examples will benefit from working through the first one or two situations in a small group. They will probably also find it easier to write hyperbole examples than examples of understatement.

- Support English language learners by working through this activity with them as a group.

- Challenge students who are ready for more by asking them to write their own situations and examples of hyperbole and understatement.

Hyperbole and Understatement

Assessment

There are various ways to assess student understanding beyond their completion of the activity sheet. Choose one or more of the following methods to evaluate their learning:

- Conduct observations while students are working.

- Ask students to write additional examples for each situation.

- Ask students to write a brief reflection about their experience of writing hyperbole and understatement. Which type of statement was easiest to write? Why?

Answer Key

Answers will vary. Accept responses that make sense and are examples of hyperbole and understatement.

Name _____ Date _____

Hyperbole and Understatement

Authors use a variety of devices to get their point across. One of the most commonly used devices is called **hyperbole.** This is a deliberate exaggeration that is meant to emphasize a point or to be funny.

Examples:

"Where were you when I explained this a million times?" is an exaggeration that makes a point.

"Your car is so old it has a place to attach the horse's harness" is an exaggeration that's also meant to be funny.

Understatement is the opposite of hyperbole and refers to a figure of speech that says less than is intended.

Here are the examples above rephrased as understatements:

"He's not the world's greatest listener."

"This car might be old, but it just needs some minor adjustments to get it back on the road."

Read the following situations. Then write two statements for each situation, one hyperbole and one understatement.

1. **Situation:** You take an important exam in class today.

   Hyperbole:

   Understatement:

(continued)

Name   Date

Hyperbole and Understatement

2. **Situation:** The outside temperature is 110 degrees.

   Hyperbole:

   Understatement:

3. **Situation:** You meet a young woman who is 6'1" tall.

   Hyperbole:

   Understatement:

4. **Situation:** You have been awake for 24 hours.

   Hyperbole:

   Understatement:

5. **Situation:** You just finished watching a 3 ½-hour movie.

   Hyperbole:

   Understatement:

Literary Paradoxes

Class Configuration

Time required:

50 minutes

Structure:

pairs (activity sheet), group (discussion)

Materials:

- 1 copy of the activity sheet for each student

Learning objectives:

- Students will discuss and answer questions about five paradox statements taken from literature.

Standards

IRA/NCTE

3. Students apply a wide range of strategies to comprehend, interpret, evaluate, and appreciate texts. They draw on their prior experience, their interactions with other readers and writers, their knowledge of word meaning and of other texts, their word identification strategies, and their understanding of textual features (e.g., sound-letter correspondence, sentence structure, context, graphics).

McREL

Language Arts: Standard 5. Uses the general skills and strategies of the reading process

Laying the Groundwork

Accessing students' prior knowledge will help them to develop new skills. Before starting this lesson, make sure students understand concepts such as the following:

- A paradox is a statement that appears to contradict itself when you first read it.

- Authors often use paradox to express an unpopular opinion or to make their readers think about an idea from a different point of view.

Students should be familiar with the following vocabulary:

paradox   a statement that appears to contradict itself when you first read it

Literary Paradoxes

Teaching Tip

Depending on available time, you may decide to have students work on the first three paradoxes in class and finish the last two on their own as homework.

Instructional Guide/Procedure

- Ask students to form pairs.

- Distribute the activity sheets.

- Review the directions and give students 35 minutes to complete the activity.

- Lead a brief class discussion about the students' responses to the questions.

- As students are responding to each paradox, remind them to do the following:

  - Focus first on the contradiction in the statement.

  - Identify the point the writer is trying to make.

  - Think about the writer's own opinion about the idea being expressed.

Supporting All Learners

- Students who are struggling with analyzing the paradox will benefit from underlining the key words that identify the contradiction first. This will help them answer the first two questions. You might ask a struggling pair to join another pair to form a group of four.

- Support English language learners by working through this activity with them as a group. You may also find it more beneficial to focus on no more than three of the paradoxes, rather than attempting to finish all five.

- Challenge students who are ready for more by asking them to write their own paradoxes.

Assessment

There are various ways to assess student understanding beyond their completion of the activity sheet. Choose one or more of the following methods to evaluate their learning:

- Conduct observations while students are working.

- During the class discussion, ask volunteers to share responses that differ, and then discuss why more than one answer may be appropriate.

- Ask students to write a brief reflection about their experience of analyzing the paradoxes.

Literary Paradoxes

Answer Key

Answers will vary, but may include the following:

1. a. that companionship would be found in solitude, which means the opposite

   b. relationships; who you spend your time with

   c. Sometimes it's better to be alone.

2. a. that copies that have been corrected could have more mistakes than copies that were left alone

   b. that there comes a time when you need to leave well enough alone

   c. He might suspect that people who spend too much time on something have hidden motives or agendas.

3. a. the use of the words *best* and *worst* to describe the same time

   b. How can things be at their best and worst at the same time?

   c. He believed that this was a time of great turmoil and that people had very divided feelings about what was happening.

4. a. the idea of dying many times before your actual death

   b. the impact of cowardly behavior on a person

   c. He doesn't respect cowards very much, but at the same time, the writer might feel pity for cowards because it must be horrible to die many times.

5. a. The people who like success the most haven't experienced it.

   b. the true value of success

   c. The writer believes that people overvalue success. She finds it isn't so pleasant once it has been achieved.

Name   Date

Literary Paradoxes

A **paradox** is a statement that appears to contradict itself when you first read it. However, after you think about what the paradox says, you see that it points to an underlying truth. Authors often use paradox to express an unpopular opinion or to make their readers think about an idea from a different point of view.

Here's an example of a paradox from George Orwell's *Animal Farm*: "All animals are equal, but some animals are more equal than others."

What is the contradiction in the example, and what is Orwell asking the reader to think about?

Read each paradox below. Discuss it with your partner, and then write your answers to the questions in the space provided.

1. **Paradox:** I never found the companion that was so companionable as solitude. (Henry David Thoreau)

   a. What is the contradiction in this paradox?

   b. What is the writer asking you to think about?

   c. What can you conclude about the writer's thoughts on this topic?

2. **Paradox:** The most corrected copies are commonly the least correct. (Francis Bacon)

   a. What is the contradiction in this paradox?

   b. What is the writer asking you to think about?

   c. What can you conclude about the writer's thoughts on this topic?

(continued)

Name _____   Date _____

Literary Paradoxes

3. **Paradox:** It was the best of times, it was the worst of times. (Charles Dickens)

   a. What is the contradiction in this paradox?

   b. What is the writer asking you to think about?

   c. What can you conclude about the writer's thoughts on this topic?

4. **Paradox:** Cowards die many times before their deaths. (William Shakespeare)

   a. What is the contradiction in this paradox?

   b. What is the writer asking you to think about?

   c. What can you conclude about the writer's thoughts on this topic?

5. **Paradox:** Success is counted sweetest by those who ne'er succeed. (Emily Dickinson)

   a. What is the contradiction in this paradox?

   b. What is the writer asking you to think about?

   c. What can you conclude about the writer's thoughts on this topic?

The Power of Symbols

Class Configuration

Time required:

50 minutes

Structure:

individual (activity sheet), group (discussion)

Materials:

- 1 copy of the novel *The House on Mango Street* by Sandra Cisneros or other assigned reading for each student

- 1 copy of the activity sheet for each student

Learning objectives:

- Students will brainstorm and categorize a list of common symbols.

- Students will identify, describe, and illustrate a symbol for a character in an assigned reading.

Standards

IRA/NCTE

3. Students apply a wide range of strategies to comprehend, interpret, evaluate, and appreciate texts. They draw on their prior experience, their interactions with other readers and writers, their knowledge of word meaning and of other texts, their word identification strategies, and their understanding of textual features (e.g., sound-letter correspondence, sentence structure, context, graphics).

McREL

Language Arts: Standard 5. Uses the general skills and strategies of the reading process

Laying the Groundwork

Accessing students' prior knowledge will help them to develop new skills. Before starting this lesson, make sure students have read the assigned text.

Students should be familiar with the following vocabulary:

symbol   something (person, place, action) that stands for something else

The Power of Symbols

Teaching Tip

This activity may be used with any text (novel, short story, play) you are assigning to students.

Instructional Guide/Procedure

- Distribute the activity sheets.

- Review the directions and give students 2–3 minutes to brainstorm a list of familiar symbols.

- Ask students to share at least one symbol from their lists. Record their responses.

- Lead a brief discussion about the list of symbols. Ask students if they can see ways these symbols might be categorized (e.g., objects, places, people). Identify categories and group the symbols.

- Review the directions on the activity sheet. Give the students 30 minutes to complete the activity.

- Close the activity by asking volunteers to share the characters and symbols they chose. Point out similarities and differences in the choices made.

- As students are completing the activity, ask them to do the following:

  - Choose a character that is especially interesting to them.

  - Brainstorm several possible symbols before selecting one.

  - Think carefully about what the selected symbol represents.

Supporting All Learners

- Students who are struggling with identifying a symbol will benefit from choosing a character and drawing a mind web of the character's attributes, likes, dislikes, and so forth. This will help the student identify an appropriate symbol.

- Support English language learners by allowing them to work in pairs. Make certain they clearly understand the pre-assigned reading, and have each pair begin by choosing a character and drawing a mind web of the character's attributes, likes, dislikes, and so forth. This will help the students identify and write about appropriate symbols.

- Challenge students who are ready for more by asking them to write a cinquain or diamante poem about the character and the selected symbol.

The Power of Symbols

Assessment

There are various ways to assess student understanding beyond their completion of the activity sheet. Choose one or more of the following methods to evaluate their learning:

- Conduct observations during class discussions and while students are working.

- During the ending class discussion, ask volunteers who chose the same characters to share symbols that differ, and explain why more than one answer may be appropriate.

- Ask students to identify a major theme in the reading assignment, and ask them to identify and describe a symbol for the theme.

Answer Key

Answers will vary. Accept any that are supported in the text.

Name _____   Date _____

The Power of Symbols

A **symbol** is something (a person, object, action) that stands for something else. For example, a bull is a symbol of strength. Use the space below to list at least five familiar symbols.

Authors often use symbols to help readers understand characters or themes in a text. Choose one of the characters from your assigned text. Based on what you've read, identify a symbol that represents this character. Write a paragraph that explains the symbol you've chosen. The paragraph must do the following:

- Identify the symbol.

- Provide a literal description of the symbol.

- Explain what the symbol represents.

- Describe how the text supports use of this symbol.

Describe your paragraph.

Analogy or Simile?

Class Configuration

Time required:

20 minutes

Structure:

individual (activity sheet), group (discussion)

Materials:

- 1 copy of the activity sheet for each student

Learning objectives:

- Students correctly identify examples of similes and analogies and explain their answers.

Standards

IRA/NCTE

3. Students apply a wide range of strategies to comprehend, interpret, evaluate, and appreciate texts. They draw on their prior experience, their interactions with other readers and writers, their knowledge of word meaning and of other texts, their word identification strategies, and their understanding of textual features (e.g., sound-letter correspondence, sentence structure, context, graphics).

McREL

Language Arts: Standard 5. Uses the general skills and strategies of the reading process

Laying the Groundwork

Accessing students' prior knowledge will help them to develop new skills. Before starting this lesson, make sure students are familiar with the following terms:

simile   a figure of speech that compares two unlike things using the words *like* or *as*

analogy   compares two different things that have something in common (Unlike a simile, an analogy may identify several points of similarity and is intended to clarify a concept or idea.)

Teaching Tip

Use this activity after students have completed the Playful Like a Snake? Nonsense Similes activity.

Analogy or Simile?

Instructional Guide/Procedure

- Distribute the activity sheets.

- Review the directions and give students 10 minutes to complete the activity.

- Close the activity by asking volunteers to share their answers and explanations.

- As students are completing the activity, ask them to do the following:

  - Refer back to the definitions for *simile* and *analogy*.

  - Use the definition for the figure of speech they use in their answers.

Supporting All Learners

- Students who are struggling with discriminating between a simile and an analogy will benefit from asking themselves, "What is the purpose of this example?" If the purpose is to clarify something, the example is probably an analogy.

- Analogies are usually very challenging for English language learners. Support these students by making certain they understand the meaning of each statement in the activity, and are clear about the purpose of an analogy. Consider working with these students in a small group.

- Challenge students who are ready for more by asking them to write 2–3 analogies to share with the class.

Assessment

There are various ways to assess student understanding beyond their completion of the activity sheet. Choose one or more of the following methods to evaluate their learning:

- Conduct observations while students are working.

- Ask students to explain the difference between a simile and an analogy in their own words, including examples.

Answer Key

1. A
2. S
3. A
4. S
5. A

Explanations may vary. Accept any that are supported by the definitions of *simile* and *analogy*.

Name _____   Date _____

Analogy or Simile?

An **analogy** is like a simile because it compares two different things that have something in common. However, unlike a simile, an analogy can identify several points of similarity and is intended to clarify a concept or idea.

Examples: Her heart was as hard as a rock. (simile)

Your heart is a muscle that works like a pump. Just as a pump moves water from one place to another, your heart moves blood from one place in your body to another. (analogy)

Authors use analogies to explain something or enhance the reader's understanding of an idea. Good analogies are short and clear. They use a familiar concept to explain the unfamiliar.

Read the statements below. Some are analogies, and others are similes. Mark each analogy with an *A* and each simile with an *S*. Then write 1 to 2 sentences explaining your answer.

_____ 1. Think of the directions for this assignment like a travel guide. Just as a travel guide is used to plan a vacation, careful reading of these directions will enable you to learn about your project options, develop an action plan, and successfully complete your project.

_____ 2. His voice was rough, like gravel.

(continued)

Name _____ Date _____

Analogy or Simile?

_____ 3. Your project is like a theatrical production. You and your work will be center stage. The teacher and your fellow students will provide backstage and technical support.

_____ 4. With three people working, the job was finished as quick as a wink.

_____ 5. What is the role of a teacher? Is it his or her job to pour facts into students' heads in the same way we fill a glass with water?

It's Not What You Think

Class Configuration

Time required:

50 minutes

Structure:

individual (activity sheet), group (discussion)

Materials:

- 1 copy of a short story that includes examples of situational irony (e.g., *The Gift of the Magi* by O'Henry or *The Necklace* by Guy de Maupassant) for each student

- 1 copy of the activity sheet for each student

Learning objectives:

- Students will identify examples of situational irony.

- After reading a short story, students will answer questions about situational irony in the reading.

Standards

IRA/NCTE

3. Students apply a wide range of strategies to comprehend, interpret, evaluate, and appreciate texts. They draw on their prior experience, their interactions with other readers and writers, their knowledge of word meaning and of other texts, their word identification strategies, and their understanding of textual features (e.g., sound-letter correspondence, sentence structure, context, graphics).

McREL

Language Arts: Standard 5. Uses the general skills and strategies of the reading process

Laying the Groundwork

Accessing students' prior knowledge will help them to develop new skills. Before starting this lesson, make sure students understand the following:

- Irony is a popular device, appearing in literature, plays, films, and music. Why do people like irony? Perhaps it is because they enjoy figuring out the true meaning of things that are said and done.

It's Not What You Think

Students should be familiar with the following vocabulary:

irony	the use of words to communicate the opposite of their exact meaning
verbal irony	occurs when a person says the opposite of what he or she means
situational irony	takes place when a person would anticipate one situation and something completely different happens
dramatic irony	the discrepancy between the facts known to a character and the facts known to the audience

Teaching Tip

This activity works well using any content that incorporates situational irony. With a few modifications to the questions on the activity sheet, you can easily adapt this lesson to focus on verbal or dramatic irony as well.

Instructional Guide/Procedure

- Distribute a copy of the activity sheet and short story to each student.

- Review the directions initial directions and give students 2–3 minutes to brainstorm an example of situational irony.

- Lead a brief 10-minute discussion about the examples students wrote on their activity sheets.

- Explain that students will now read a story that relies heavily on situational irony. Ask students to highlight examples they find as they read the story, and tell them to answer the questions on the activity sheet once they've finished reading. Give students 35 minutes to complete the activity.

- As students are completing the activity, remind them to do the folllowing:

  - Take the time to highlight the story as they read.

  - To pay close attention to strategies the author uses to lead the reader's thinking.

  - To think about alternative ways the story might end.

It's Not What You Think

Supporting All Learners

- Students who will struggle with this activity will benefit from reading the story ahead of time. Assign the reading the day before you plan to use this activity.

- Support English language learners by allowing them to read and discuss the story as a group. Each student should write his or her own answers to the questions, but you may encourage the group to come to a consensus before individual members begin writing.

- Challenge students who are ready for more by asking them to revise the story using the ending the author wants readers to anticipate.

Assessment

There are various ways to assess student understanding beyond their completion of the activity sheet. Choose one or more of the following methods to evaluate their learning:

- Conduct observations while the students are working.

- Lead a class discussion of the students' answers to the questions on the activity sheet, asking students to share their answers and explain their thinking.

- Have students write a reflection about which ending they prefer (the anticipated or actual ending), and why.

Answer Key

Answers will vary, depending upon the story used. Accept answers that are supported in the text that students read.

Name _____   Date _____

It's Not What You Think

Irony is the use of words to communicate the opposite of their exact meaning. Three kinds of irony are used most often.

- **Verbal irony** occurs when a person says the opposite of what he or she means.

- **Situational irony** takes place when a person anticipates one situation, and something completely different happens.

- **Dramatic irony** is the discrepancy between the facts known to a character and the facts known to the audience.

A common example of situational irony is the surprise ending for a book, movie, or song. This is because things don't turn out the way you think they will. Think of an example of a surprise ending and write it below.

Read the short story provided by your teacher. As you're reading, highlight any examples of situational irony you may find. When you finish the story, answer the following questions.

1. What does the author want the reader to think will happen? Support your answer with references from the text.

(continued)

Name _____   Date _____

It's Not What You Think

2. What actually happens in the story? Support your answer with references from the text.

3. How would things be different if the ending the reader anticipates actually happened? Support your answer with references from the text.

A Rose by Any Other Name

Class Configuration

Time required:

20 minutes

Structure:

trios (activity sheet), group (discussion)

Materials:

- 1 copy of the activity sheet for each student

- *Optional:* a list of clichés for students who might have difficulty coming up with their own (www.clichesite.com)

Learning objectives:

- Students will brainstorm a list of 12–15 clichés.

- Students will rewrite four of these clichés.

Standards

IRA/NCTE

3. Students apply a wide range of strategies to comprehend, interpret, evaluate, and appreciate texts. They draw on their prior experience, their interactions with other readers and writers, their knowledge of word meaning and of other texts, their word identification strategies, and their understanding of textual features (e.g., sound-letter correspondence, sentence structure, context, graphics).

McREL

Language Arts: Standard 5. Uses the general skills and strategies of the reading process

Laying the Groundwork

Accessing students' prior knowledge will help them to develop new skills. Before starting this lesson, make sure students understand the following:

- Clichés are overused expressions.

- You may want to provide several examples of clichés to ensure that students clearly understand what they are.

A Rose by Any Other Name

Students should be familiar with the following vocabulary:

cliché   an expression that was once powerful or catchy, but has become so overused that it has lost its punch (Examples: "hope springs eternal" or "grasping at straws")

Teaching Tip

Students often use clichés in their writing. It's important that they understand there's nothing wrong with the ideas expressed in different clichés. The reason these phrases become trite is that they say something well. Help students understand that you want them to enhance their reading and writing by taking a good idea and rephrasing it so it is fresh.

Extend or enhance the activity by starting a class list of revised clichés for creative writing.

Instructional Guide/Procedure

- Ask students to form groups of three, and distribute a copy of the activity sheet to each student.

- Review the directions on the activity sheet. Spend time reviewing the examples provided, making sure that students understand the task. (5 minutes)

- Have groups brainstorm a list of 12–15 clichés. (10 minutes)

- Ask a few volunteers to share some of the clichés their group listed. Check to make sure that each group has at least four clichés per group member.

- Have each group member select at least three clichés from that group's list, and rewrite those clichés following the directions on the activity sheet.

- Ask a few volunteers to share some of the clichés they revised.

- As students are completing the activity, remind them to do the following:

  - Follow the directions in each column heading.

  - Use a thesaurus to find possible synonyms.

  - Remember that they are looking for a word or a phrase that denotes something else, but can be used in place of prepositional phrases they list.

Adolescent Literacy: Figurative Language

A Rose by Any Other Name

Supporting All Learners

- Students who are struggling with this activity will benefit from being given a few clichés to start their brainstorming list. It will also be helpful for you to work through one revision with them before having them rewrite on their own.

- Support English language learners by leading them through this activity as a group. You may need to provide 2–3 clichés, and then help the group make revisions.

- Challenge students who are ready for more by asking them to explain the title of this lesson.

Assessment

There are various ways to assess student understanding beyond their completion of the activity sheet. Choose one or more of the following methods to evaluate their learning:

- Conduct observations while students are working.

- Ask students to write a short reflection describing their thought process as they completed this activity.

Answer Key

Answers will vary. Accept responses that make sense and comply with the directions.

Name _____ Date _____

A Rose by Any Other Name

A **cliché** is an expression that was once powerful or catchy, but has become so overused that it has lost its punch. Familiar phrases such as "hope springs eternal" or "grasping at straws" are examples. There's nothing wrong with the ideas expressed in different clichés; the reason these phrases become trite is that they say something well. The problem is that the phrases are too familiar; people don't pay much attention to them when they read.

In this activity, your group will use the chart below to brainstorm 12 to 15 clichés (you need at least 12). After a brief class discussion, group members will each choose at least 4 of the clichés from the list and then rewrite them.

Cliché	This cliché means . . .	Rewritten cliché
Example: Rome wasn't built in a day.	Example: It takes time for big things to happen.	Example: Be patient. Important tasks take time.

Buzz Words

Class Configuration

Time required:

40–50 minutes

Structure:

individual (activity sheet), group (discussion)

Materials:

- 1 copy for each student of one or more comic strips (or panels) that can be described using onomatopoeia. (Use newspapers, comic books or online sources such as www.comics.com. Depending upon the illustration, you may want to cover up dialogue and definitely need to cover up existing onomatopoeia captions.)

- 1 copy of the activity sheet for each student

Learning objectives:

- Students will brainstorm a list of onomatopoeia words.

- Students will use onomatopoeia to describe what's happening in comic panels provided by the teacher.

- Students will draw a picture and write a caption for it using onomatopoeia words not used in the second activity.

Standards

IRA/NCTE

6. Students apply knowledge of language structure, language conventions (e.g., spelling and punctuation), media techniques, figurative language, and genre to create, critique, and discuss print and non-print texts.

McREL

Language Arts: Standard 2. Uses the stylistic and rhetorical aspects of writing

Buzz Words

Laying the Groundwork

Accessing students' prior knowledge will help them to develop new skills. Before starting this lesson, make sure students understand the definition of *onomatopoeia,* and how these words are used to describe action in a comic.

Students should be familiar with the following vocabulary:

onomatopoeia   the use of words which, when spoken, sound like what they mean, such as *hiss, slurp,* or *splat*

Teaching Tip

This activity can be repeated multiple times using different comic strips or panels. Encourage students to use different words each time, to increase their onomatopoeia vocabulary.

Instructional Guide/Procedure

- Distribute the activity sheets and comic strips or panels.

- Review the definition of *onomatopoeia* and give students 2–3 minutes to brainstorm a list of at least 10 words.

- Ask students to share at least one word from their lists. Record their responses to start building a class list of onomatopoeia words.

- Review the directions on the activity sheet. Give the students 5–10 minutes to describe the action in the comic strip or panel you provided.

- Finally, give students 15–20 minutes to draw and write captions for their own pictures. Remind them they may not repeat onomatopoeia words used to describe the comic strip or panel.

- As students are completing the activity, ask them to do the following:

  - Continue to add onomatopoeia words to their brainstorming list. This will help them expand beyond the obvious words.

  - Use several onomatopoeia words in their descriptions of the comic strip or panel.

  - Think carefully about the picture they will draw so that the action can be reflected in words they did not use when describing the comic.

Buzz Words

Supporting All Learners

- Students who are struggling with brainstorming a list of onomatopoeia words will benefit from paying attention during the class discussion. Encourage them to add words to their lists as other students share. It may also be helpful for these students to begin the second activity by writing a caption for the comic, and then writing a more complete description.

- Support English language learners by encouraging them to brainstorm a list of onomatopoeia words in their native language and then translate them into English. You may need to prompt them at first (e.g., What sound does a chicken make? How does a bell sound?).

- Challenge students who are ready for more by asking them to find comic strips or other print material that uses onomatopoeia and bring these examples to class.

Assessment

There are various ways to assess student understanding beyond their completion of the activity sheet. Choose one or more of the following methods to evaluate their learning:

- Conduct observations during class discussions and while students are working.

- Ask students to write a reflection in which they coin at least one onomatopoeia word of their own.

Answer Key

Answers will vary. Accept all reasonable responses.

Name _____   Date _____

Buzz Words

Onomatopoeia is the use of words which, when spoken, sound like what they mean, such as *hiss, slurp,* or *splat.*

1. Brainstorm a list of at least 10 onomatopoeia words.

2. Onomatopoeia is frequently used in comics to describe the action in a panel. Look at the comics provided by your teacher. Use onomatopoeia to describe what's happening in each picture.

3. On the back of this sheet, draw your own picture and write a caption for it using onomatopoeia. You may not use the same words you used to describe the comics.

Sally Sells Seashells

Class Configuration

Time required:

30 minutes

Structure:

groups of 4–6 students (activity sheet)

Materials:

- 1 copy of the activity sheet for each student

- a dictionary and a thesaurus for each group (hard copy or online)

Learning objectives:

- Students will increase their vocabularies by creating categorized lists of words that begin with an assigned letter. The word lists will be used in a subsequent activity.

- Students will use their word lists to write five examples of alliteration.

Standards

IRA/NCTE

6. Students apply knowledge of language structure, language conventions (e.g., spelling and punctuation), media techniques, figurative language, and genre to create, critique, and discuss print and non-print texts.

McREL

Language Arts: Standard 2. Uses the stylistic and rhetorical aspects of writing

Laying the Groundwork

Accessing students' prior knowledge will help them develop new skills. Before starting this lesson, make sure students are comfortable using a dictionary and a thesaurus.

Students should be familiar with the following vocabulary:

alliteration   the repetition of consonant sounds, usually at the beginning of a word

Sally Sells Seashells

Teaching Tip

The initial letters chosen for this activity are the five most common. However, you may add additional letters for more variety. If you decide to do this, have students work in smaller groups or pairs.

Instructional Guide/Procedure

- Divide students into groups of 4–6 students.

- Distribute the activity sheets.

- Review the directions. Assign a letter to each group, and give students 10 minutes to make their lists of nouns, verbs, adjectives, and adverbs that start with their assigned letter.

- Check to make sure that each group has made their lists, and then give the groups 10 minutes to write their examples of alliteration.

- As students are completing the activity, ask them to do the following:

  - Choose words that will make their examples more interesting.

  - Use a dictionary or a thesaurus to expand their lists beyond obvious or common words.

  - Think about ways to make their examples even more memorable.

Supporting All Learners

- Students who are struggling with this activity need to work with a dictionary or a thesaurus from the beginning. The group structure should provide additional support for these students.

- Support English language learners by monitoring their groups to check for understanding. You may want to walk through this activity once with these students before having them work more independently.

- Challenge students who are ready for more by asking them to find and bring to class 3–5 real-world examples of alliteration.

Sally Sells Seashells

Assessment

There are various ways to assess student understanding beyond their completion of the activity sheet. Choose one or more of the following methods to evaluate their learning:

- Conduct observations while students are working.

- Quiz students on their ability to complete this activity individually by giving the class a letter and asking them to write alliteration examples on their own.

- Ask students to write a reflection about why they think advertisers use alliteration.

Answer Key

Answers will vary. Accept word lists and examples that meet the criteria described in the directions.

Name _____   Date _____

Sally Sells Seashells

Alliteration is the repetition of consonant sounds, usually at the beginning of words. Writers use alliteration to link words or to establish rhythm. For example, think about your favorite poems from childhood. Are the writings of Dr. Seuss on your list? His books often use alliteration throughout the text.

Alliteration is also used as a mnemonic device—words or expressions designed to help people remember something. This is why news headlines, advertisements, buzzwords, character names, and literary titles often use alliteration. Here are a few examples:

Headline: Baby Boomers Bite the Bullet on Health Costs

Advertisement: Don't Dream It. Drive It.

Buzzword: hip hop

Character name: Bilbo Baggins

Book title: *Sense and Sensibility*

The five most commonly used first letters in the English language are *t, o, a, w,* and *b.* Your teacher will assign one of these letters to your group. Brainstorm a list of words that start with your assigned letter, five for each word category.

Nouns	Verbs	Adjectives	Adverbs
_____	_____	_____	_____
_____	_____	_____	_____
_____	_____	_____	_____
_____	_____	_____	_____
_____	_____	_____	_____

(continued)

Name _____   Date _____

Sally Sells Seashells

Use the words from your list to write your own examples of alliteration below.

Headline:

Advertisement:

Buzzword:

Character name:

Book title:

Be on the lookout for real-world examples of alliteration. Now you know that someone is trying to grab your attention and make you remember something!

TEACHER PAGE

Almost Seems Human

Class Configuration

Time required:

50 minutes

Structure:

individual (activity sheet), group (discussion)

Materials:

- 1 copy of a poem for each student that includes several examples of personification such as *Mirror* by Sylvia Plath or *Once by the Pacific* by Robert Frost

- 1 copy of the activity sheet for each student

- 1 sheet of writing paper for each student

Learning objectives:

- Students will identify vocabulary used in a poem to personify an animal, idea, or inanimate object.

- Students will use pairs of nouns and verbs to write a personification poem.

Standards

IRA/NCTE

6. Students apply knowledge of language structure, language conventions (e.g., spelling and punctuation), media techniques, figurative language, and genre to create, critique, and discuss print and non-print texts.

McREL

Language Arts: Standard 2. Uses the stylistic and rhetorical aspects of writing

Laying the Groundwork

Accessing students' prior knowledge will help them to develop new skills. Before starting this lesson, make sure students understand the following:

- Authors use personification to capture readers' interest and help them visualize the text.

- Personification frequently appears in poetry.

- The poet's choice of vocabulary impacts the power of the language used and the reader's ability to visualize the poem.

Almost Seems Human

Students should be familiar with the following vocabulary:

personification   the attribution of human characteristics to animals, ideas, objects, etc.

Teaching Tip

This activity works well using any poem that employs personification. For additional examples, visit your library or conduct an online search using the keywords "personification poetry."

Instructional Guide/Procedure

- Distribute a copy of the poem, the activity sheet, and a sheet of writing paper to each student. Make sure students immediately put their names on the activity sheets.

- Review the directions for Activity 1.

- Read the poem out loud and lead a discussion about the figurative language used by the poet to achieve personification. (15 minutes)

- Review the directions for Activity 2. Give students 5 minutes to make their lists on nouns and verbs.

- Have students exchange papers. Give them 5 minutes to make noun/verb pairs using the lists.

- Have students exchange papers again. (No student should have his or her own paper.) Give them 5 minutes to review the ten noun/verb pairs and choose five.

- Give students 15 minutes to draft a personification poem using the five noun/verb pairs they selected.

- As students are completing the activity, ask them to do the following:

  - Identify at least three examples of personification in the poem you read to the class.

  - Choose interesting noun/verb pairs that may not seem well-aligned at first.

  - Think about multiple ways these word pairs could be put together before writing the draft poem.

Almost Seems Human

Supporting All Learners

- Students who are struggling with this activity can start making their noun and verb lists using the text of the poem that's read aloud. Making and choosing noun/verb pairs should not pose a problem. It may help to create a mind map or draw a picture showing how the noun/verb pairs could connect before these students begin drafting a poem.

- Support English language learners by allowing them to work through this activity in pairs. Make sure they understand the meaning of the nouns and verbs in the word pairs.

- Challenge students who are ready for more by providing a poetry anthology and asking them to find 2–3 additional examples of personification. Make sure these students are able to explain their choices.

Assessment

There are various ways to assess student understanding beyond their completion of the activity sheet. Choose one or more of the following methods to evaluate their learning:

- Conduct observations while students are working.

- Provide a copy of a different short poem that uses personification. Ask students to identify what is being personified and to support their answers by highlighting the words and phrases used for personification.

Answer Key

Answers will vary. Accept poems that meet the criteria described in the lesson directions.

Name _____ Date _____

Almost Seems Human

Personification is the attribution of human characteristics to animals, ideas, objects, and so forth. Authors use personification to make descriptions more interesting. For example, which of these sample sentences is more likely to grab someone's attention?

1. During the storm, the wind blew really hard.

2. The house trembled as the howling gale punched at the doors and rattled the windows.

Poets often use personification in their writing.

Activity 1

Follow along as your teacher reads the poem distributed with this activity sheet. As you listen, underline words and phrases used by the poet to personify an idea, an animal, or an inanimate object. Participate in the class discussion about the vocabulary used by the poet.

Activity 2

Step 1: Write a list of ten nouns (animals, objects, ideas) and ten verbs below.

Nouns   **Verbs**

Step 2: Give your list to a classmate sitting next to you. Take the list a classmate gives you and read the list of nouns and verbs. Draw lines to connect each noun to a verb. As much as possible, make the word pairs interesting.

(continued)

www.walch.com

Name _____   Date _____

Almost Seems Human

Step 3: Give this list to a classmate sitting next to you, but not the person who originally wrote the list. Take the word pairs a classmate gives you and read the ten pairs of nouns and verbs (you may not use the list you wrote originally). Choose five word pairs and write a personification poem that uses these word pairs. Write your poem in the space below.

Contradicting Yourself?

Class Configuration

Time required:

25 minutes

Structure:

groups of 3–5 students (activity sheet), total class (discussion)

Materials:

- 1 copy of the activity sheet for each student

Learning objectives:

- Students will identify four examples of familiar oxymora.

- Students will write three original oxymora.

Standards

IRA/NCTE

6. Students apply knowledge of language structure, language conventions (e.g., spelling and punctuation), media techniques, figurative language, and genre to create, critique, and discuss print and non-print texts.

McREL

Language Arts: Standard 2. Uses the stylistic and rhetorical aspects of writing

Laying the Groundwork

Accessing students' prior knowledge will help them to develop new skills. Before starting this lesson, make sure students understand the following:

- Writers often pair seemingly contradictory words to be funny or to emphasize the contradiction.

- Use of this type of figurative language helps readers understand and remember the point being made by the writer.

Students should be familiar with the following vocabulary:

oxymoron   a figure of speech that includes an apparent contradiction

Contradicting Yourself?

Teaching Tip

This kind of humor is usually very appealing to teens. You can extend or enhance the lesson by asking students to find or create additional oxymora, and share them with other students.

Instructional Guide/Procedure

- Divide the class into small groups and distribute a copy of the activity sheet to each student.

- Review the directions on the activity sheet and ask the groups to brainstorm at least four familiar oxymora. (5 minutes)

- Ask each group to share at least one oxymoron from their list. (5 minutes)

- Ask individual group members to each write three original oxymora, share with their groups, and select three to share with the class. (10 minutes)

- Have each group share the three oxymora they selected. (5 minutes)

- As students are completing the activity, ask them to do the following:

  - Encourage group discussion while brainstorming familiar oxymora.

  - Remember that it might be easiest to use a noun and adjective when writing an original oxymoron.

  - Be prepared to explain why the group chose the three oxymora they plan to share with the class.

Supporting All Learners

- The group structure will benefit students who are struggling with this activity. If you have access to the Internet, you may want to allow these students to search for and record oxymora they find.

- The contradictions may be very difficult for English language learners to understand. Support these students by working through this activity with them as a group. If possible, ask native speakers of your students' primary languages to provide examples of oxymora in those languages.

- Challenge students who are ready for more by asking them to review the oxymora selected by the groups, and choose the top five to use in a PowerPoint presentation that explains oxymora.

Contradicting Yourself?

Assessment

There are various ways to assess student understanding beyond their completion of the activity sheet. Choose one or more of the following methods to evaluate their learning:

- Conduct observations while students are working.

- Ask students to write a brief reflection explaining their group's choices for the three oxymora they shared with the class.

Answer Key

Answers will vary. Accept responses that are oxymora.

Name _____   Date _____

Contradicting Yourself?

An **oxymoron** is a figure of speech that includes an apparent contradiction.

> Examples:
>
> jumbo shrimp
>
> double solitaire
>
> silent scream
>
> virtual reality
>
> blinding light

Some oxymora are used to be humorous, such as customer service or cafeteria food. Other oxymora are intended to emphasize a contradiction, such as *act naturally* or *passive aggressive*.

Oxymora are nearly always a combination of a noun and an adjective. Work with your group to brainstorm a list of at least four familiar oxymora. List them below.

Now write three original oxymora.

Share your original oxymora with your group members. As a group, choose three and write them below.

Translating Doublespeak

Class Configuration

Time required:

25 minutes

Structure:

pairs (activity sheet), group (discussion)

Materials:

- 1 copy of the activity sheet for each student

Learning objectives:

- Students will "translate" twelve examples of doublespeak.

Standards

IRA/NCTE

3. Students apply a wide range of strategies to comprehend, interpret, evaluate, and appreciate texts. They draw on their prior experience, their interactions with other readers and writers, their knowledge of word meaning and of other texts, their word identification strategies, and their understanding of textual features (e.g., sound-letter correspondence, sentence structure, context, graphics).

McREL

Language Arts: Standard 5. Uses the general skills and strategies of the reading process

Laying the Groundwork

Accessing students' prior knowledge will help them to develop new skills. Before starting this lesson, make sure students understand that people often use euphemisms when they are uncomfortable with speaking plainly, or when they must say something, but can't (or won't) say it directly. Corporations, governmental agencies, and military organizations often fall into this second category, using doublespeak in an effort to say something without really saying anything.

Students should be familiar with the following vocabulary:

euphemism   use of an inoffensive word or phrase to express something that people often find uncomfortable or embarrassing to say

doublespeak   language that is deliberately designed to disguise its real meaning using euphemism

Translating Doublespeak

Teaching Tip

This activity can be expanded or enhanced by encouraging students to collect examples of doublespeak from newspaper and magazine articles or online, and then using these terms to write a poem or lyrics for a song.

Instructional Guide/Procedure

- Ask students to form pairs and distribute a copy of the activity sheet to each student.

- Review the directions at the top of the activity sheet. Spend time reviewing the examples provided, making sure that students understand the task. (5 minutes)

- Have pairs write the meaning of each doublespeak example. (15 minutes)

- Ask a few volunteers to share some of the meanings they wrote. (5 minutes)

- As students are completing the activity, remind them to do the following:

  - Think about the literal meaning of the doublespeak words/phrases.

  - Remember the context (corporate, government, or military).

  - Base the meaning on previous experience and knowledge.

Supporting All Learners

- Students who are struggling with this activity will benefit from working through one or more examples with assistance before finishing the activity with a partner.

- Support English language learners by leading them through this activity as a group. You may need to provide an example of each doublespeak term used in a sentence where the context will help the students determine the meaning.

- Challenge students who are ready for more by asking them to coin three doublespeak terms related to school.

Adolescent Literacy: Figurative Language

Translating Doublespeak

Assessment

There are various ways to assess student understanding beyond their completion of the activity sheet. Choose one or more of the following methods to evaluate their learning:

- Conduct observations while students are working.

- Ask students to use each doublespeak term in a sentence.

- Have students find and bring to class 2–3 examples of doublespeak they hear or read.

Answer Key

Responses may vary slightly, but should include the following information:

Corporate Doublespeak	Meaning
make redundant	lay-off or fire
replacement workers	strike breakers
negative contributions to profits	lost money
orderly transition between career changes	unemployed
Government Doublespeak	**Meaning**
budget surplus	profit
special interests	representatives or lobbyists for large corporations or powerful groups (e.g., oil, National Rifle Association)
regime change	removal, by force, of an existing government.
death tax	estate tax
Military Doublespeak	**Meaning**
collateral damage	killing of innocent by-standers
friendly fire	accidental attack by allies
pre-hostility	peace
asymmetric warfare	conflict in which opposing sides are greatly mismatched (The weaker side generally resorts to guerilla tactics to stay in the fight.)

Name _____   Date _____

Translating Doublespeak

A **euphemism** is use of an inoffensive word or phrase to express something that people often find uncomfortable or embarrassing to say. Familiar euphemisms include the following:

Euphemism	Meaning
pass away	died
gone to heaven	died
washroom	toilet/bathroom
not the sharpest tool in the shed	not very smart

Doublespeak is language deliberately designed to disguise its real meaning using euphemism. Corporations, governmental agencies, and military organizations often use doublespeak. For example, the corporate term *downsize* usually means "to fire."

In this activity, you and your partner will use the chart on the next page to write the real meaning of the doublespeak words and phrases provided.

(continued)

Name _____   Date _____

Translating Doublespeak

Corporate Doublespeak	Meaning
make redundant	
replacement workers	
negative contributions to profits	
orderly transition between career changes	
Government Doublespeak	**Meaning**
budget surplus	
special interests	
regime change	
death tax	
Military Doublespeak	**Meaning**
collateral damage	
friendly fire	
pre-hostility	
asymmetric warfare	

Speaking Indirectly to Make a Point

Class Configuration

Time required:

20 minutes

Structure:

individual (activity sheet), group (discussion)

Materials:

- 1 copy of the activity sheet for each student

Learning objectives:

- Students will "translate" ten examples of litotes.

Standards

IRA/NCTE

3. Students apply a wide range of strategies to comprehend, interpret, evaluate, and appreciate texts. They draw on their prior experience, their interactions with other readers and writers, their knowledge of word meaning and of other texts, their word identification strategies, and their understanding of textual features (e.g., sound-letter correspondence, sentence structure, context, graphics).

McREL

Language Arts: Standard 5. Uses the general skills and strategies of the reading process

Laying the Groundwork

Accessing students' prior knowledge will help them to develop new skills. Before starting this lesson, make sure students understand the following:

- People sometimes speak indirectly to make a point. This figure of speech is called *litotes*.

- Litotes can trip you up when you're reading, if you aren't paying close enough attention.

Students should be familiar with the following vocabulary:

litotes	a figure of speech in which the speaker emphasizes the magnitude of a statement by denying its opposite (Example: "That dessert isn't half bad," actually means, "That dessert is really good.")
double negative	use of two negative words to make a strong positive statement

Speaking Indirectly to Make a Point

Teaching Tip

This activity can be expanded or enhanced by encouraging students to find examples of litotes in their reading and sharing them with the class.

Instructional Guide/Procedure

- Distribute a copy of the activity sheet to each student.

- Review the directions at the top of the activity sheet. Spend time reviewing the examples provided, making sure that students understand the task. (5 minutes)

- Have students write the meaning of the litotes examples. (10 minutes)

- Ask a few volunteers to share some of the meanings they wrote. (5 minutes)

- As students are completing the activity, remind them to do the following:

  - Read each example carefully.

  - Identify the double negative (e.g., not half bad, no small amount, etc.).

  - Base the meaning on the understanding that the speaker is being indirect.

Supporting All Learners

- Students who are struggling with this activity will benefit from working through one or more examples with assistance before finishing the activity with a partner.

- Support English language learners by leading them through this activity as a group.

- Challenge students who are ready for more by asking them to write three litotes to describe their feelings about school.

Assessment

There are various ways to assess student understanding beyond their completion of the activity sheet. Choose one or more of the following methods to evaluate their learning:

- Conduct observations while students are working.

- Ask students to write a reflection about why litotes are an effective figure of speech.

Speaking Indirectly to Make a Point

Answer Key

Responses may vary slightly, but should include the following information:

Litotes	Meaning
I was not a little upset.	I was very upset.
That's nothing to sneeze at.	Very important
She's no dummy!	She's intelligent.
This is no small accomplishment.	This is a big accomplishment.
That's not a bad idea.	This is a good idea.
That's no small amount of money.	That is a large amount of money.
Our plan is not unsuccessful.	Our plan worked.
I am not unhappy about the results.	I am happy about what happened.
It was no big deal.	It was not important.
It's not unusual.	It's very common.

Name _____   Date _____

Speaking Indirectly to Make a Point

Litotes is a figure of speech in which the speaker emphasizes the magnitude of a statement by denying its opposite. For example, "That dessert isn't half bad," actually means, "That dessert is really good." When reading litotes, it is important to pay close attention so you understand the speaker's true meaning

   Read the litotes in the table below and write the speaker's meaning in the space provided.

Litotes	Meaning
I was not a little upset.	
That's nothing to sneeze at.	
She's no dummy!	
This is no small accomplishment.	
That's not a bad idea.	
That's no small amount of money.	
Our plan is not unsuccessful.	
I am not unhappy about the results.	
It was no big deal.	
It's not unusual.	

TEACHER PAGE

Metaphors As Verbs

Class Configuration

Time required:

20 minutes

Structure:

pairs (activity sheet), group (discussion)

Materials:

- 1 copy of the activity sheet for each student

Learning objectives:

- Students will write three sentences using metaphors as verbs.

Standards

IRA/NCTE

6. Students apply knowledge of language structure, language conventions (e.g., spelling and punctuation), media techniques, figurative language, and genre to create, critique, and discuss print and non-print texts.

McREL

Language Arts: Standard 2. Uses the stylistic and rhetorical aspects of writing

Laying the Groundwork

Accessing students' prior knowledge will help them to develop new skills. Before starting this lesson, make sure students understand the following:

- Similes and metaphors are similar, but not identical.

- Writers use metaphors because they make language more interesting, encourage interpretation, and make it easier to write about complex emotions or ideas.

Student should be familiar with the following vocabulary:

simile	a figure of speech that compares two unlike things using the words *like* or *as*
metaphor	a figure of speech in which a word or phrase that denotes one thing is used in place of another to suggest a similarity between them

Adolescent Literacy: Figurative Language

Metaphors As Verbs

Teaching Tip

Metaphors are complex and can take many forms. This activity is one of three in which students are asked to write metaphors as different parts of speech. Do not be surprised if your students find this more challenging than you might think. However, taking the time to explore metaphors from three different angles will help your students increase their skills in writing and comprehending this type of figurative language.

Instructional Guide/Procedure

- Ask students to pair up and distribute a copy of the activity sheet to each student.

- Review the directions on the activity sheet. Spend time reviewing the examples provided, making sure that students understand the task. (10 minutes)

- Have students work in pairs to write three original metaphors. (10 minutes)

- As students are completing the activity, remind them to do the following:

  - Follow the directions in each column heading.

  - Use a thesaurus to find possible synonyms.

  - Remember that they are looking for a word or phrase that denotes something else, but can be used in place of verbs they list.

Supporting All Learners

- Students who are struggling with this activity will benefit from brainstorming a list of 8–10 verbs, and then choosing three they will be able to substitute. It may also be helpful to allow these students to work in small groups instead of pairs.

- Support English language learners by allowing them to work through this activity as a group. You may want to give these students a list of verbs and help them brainstorm substitute words.

- Challenge students who are ready for more by asking them to find examples of metaphors as verbs and bring them to share with the class.

Metaphors As Verbs

Assessment

There are various ways to assess student understanding beyond their completion of the activity sheet. Choose one or more of the following methods to evaluate their learning:

- Conduct observations while students are working.

- Ask students to write a short reflection describing their thought process as they completed this activity.

Answer Key

Answers will vary. Accept metaphors that meet the criteria described in the directions.

Name _____ Date _____

Metaphors As Verbs

A **metaphor** is a figure of speech in which a word or phrase that denotes one thing is used in place of another to suggest a similarity between them. For example, instead of saying, "He's a smart boy," the metaphor "He's a smart cookie," can be used to describe someone.

It is easy to confuse metaphors with similes. It helps to remember that metaphors do not use the words *like* or *as*. Writers use metaphors because they make language more interesting, encourage interpretation, and make it easier to write about complex emotions or ideas.

One way to increase your appreciation of metaphors is to experiment with writing them in different forms. In this particular activity, you will try writing a few metaphors as verbs. Here is an example.

Choose a verb and write it in this column.	Choose a word or phrase that denotes something else, but can be used in place of the verb in the first column.	Write your metaphor.
run	thunder	The giant thundered down the hallway, pursuing his prey.
win	hammer	Our football team is hammering the visiting team.
defeat	crush	Work responsibilities crushed Edgar.

(continued)

www.walch.com

Name _____   Date _____

Metaphors As Verbs

Now it's your turn. Complete this table to write three of your own metaphors.

Choose a verb and write it in this column.	Choose a word or phrase that denotes something else, but can be used in place of the verb in the first column.	Write your metaphor.

Adolescent Literacy: Figurative Language

Metaphors As Adjectives

Class Configuration

Time required:

20 minutes

Structure:

pairs (activity sheet), group (discussion)

Materials:

- 1 copy of the activity sheet for each student

Learning objectives:

- Students will write three sentences using metaphors as adjectives.

Standards

IRA/NCTE

6. Students apply knowledge of language structure, language conventions (e.g., spelling and punctuation), media techniques, figurative language, and genre to create, critique, and discuss print and non-print texts.

McREL

Language Arts: Standard 2. Uses the stylistic and rhetorical aspects of writing

Laying the Groundwork

Accessing students' prior knowledge will help them to develop new skills. Before starting this lesson, make sure students understand the following:

- Similes and metaphors are similar, but not identical.

- Writers use metaphors because they make language more interesting, encourage interpretation, and make it easier to write about complex emotions or ideas.

Students should be familiar with the following vocabulary:

simile	a figure of speech that compares two unlike things using the words *like* or *as*
metaphor	a figure of speech in which a word or phrase that denotes one thing is used in place of another to suggest a similarity between them

Metaphors As Adjectives

Teaching Tip

Metaphors are complex and can take many forms. This activity is one of three in which students are asked to write metaphors as different parts of speech. Do not be surprised if your students find this more challenging than you might think. However, taking the time to explore metaphors from three different angles will help your students increase their skills in writing and comprehending this type of figurative language.

Instructional Guide/Procedure

- Ask students to pair up and distribute a copy of the activity sheet to each student.

- Review the directions on the activity sheet. Spend time reviewing the examples provided, making sure that students understand the task. (10 minutes)

- Have students work in pairs to write three original metaphors. (10 minutes)

- As students are completing the activity, remind them to do the following:

  - Follow the directions in each column heading.

  - Use a thesaurus to find possible synonyms.

  - Remember that they are looking for a word or phrase that denotes something else, but can be used in place of adjectives they list.

Supporting All Learners

- Students who are struggling with this activity will benefit from brainstorming a list of 8–10 adjectives, and then choosing three they will be able to substitute. It may also be helpful to allow these students to work in small groups instead of pairs.

- Support English language learners by allowing them to work through this activity as a group. You may want to give these students a list of adjectives and help them brainstorm substitute words.

- Challenge students who are ready for more by asking them to find examples of metaphors as adjectives and bring them to share with the class.

Metaphors As Adjectives

Assessment

There are various ways to assess student understanding beyond their completion of the activity sheet. Choose one or more of the following methods to evaluate their learning:

- Conduct observations while students are working.

- Ask students to write a short reflection describing their thought process as they completed this activity.

Answer Key

Answers will vary. Accept metaphors that meet the criteria described in the directions.

Name _____   Date _____

Metaphors As Adjectives

A **metaphor** is a figure of speech in which a word or phrase that denotes one thing is used in place of another to suggest a similarity between them. For example, instead of saying, "She is a sweet girl," the metaphor "She is a peach," can be used to describe someone.

It is easy to confuse metaphors with similes. It helps to remember that metaphors do not use the words *like* or *as*. Writers use metaphors because they make language more interesting, encourage interpretation, and make it easier to write about complex emotions or ideas.

One way to increase your appreciation of metaphors is to experiment with writing them in different forms. In this particular activity, you will try writing a few metaphors as adjectives. Here is an example.

Choose an adjective and write it in this column.	Choose a word or phrase that denotes something else, but can be used in place of the adjective in the first column.	Write your metaphor.
blonde	corn silk	Her corn silk hair gleamed in the sun.
bad	volcanic	Mia's volcanic temper can be worrisome.
clever	splashy	The splashy presentation caught everyone's attention.

(continued)

Name _____   Date _____

Metaphors As Adjectives

Now it's your turn. Complete this table to write three of your own metaphors.

Choose an adjective and write it in this column.	Choose a word or phrase that denotes something else, but can be used in place of the adjective in the first column.	Write your metaphor.

Metaphors As Prepositional Phrases

Class Configuration

Time required:

20 minutes

Structure:

pairs (activity sheet), group (discussion)

Materials:

- 1 copy of the activity sheet for each student

Learning objectives:

- Students will write three sentences using metaphors as prepositional phrases.

Standards

IRA/NCTE

6. Students apply knowledge of language structure, language conventions (e.g., spelling and punctuation), media techniques, figurative language, and genre to create, critique, and discuss print and non-print texts.

McREL

Language Arts: Standard 2. Uses the stylistic and rhetorical aspects of writing

Laying the Groundwork

Accessing students' prior knowledge will help them to develop new skills. Before starting this lesson, make sure students understand the following:

- Similes and metaphors are similar, but not identical.

- Writers use metaphors because they make language more interesting, encourage interpretation, and make it easier to write about complex emotions or ideas.

Students should be familiar with the following vocabulary:

simile	a figure of speech that compares two unlike things using the words *like* or *as*
metaphor	a figure of speech in which a word or phrase that denotes one thing is used in place of another to suggest a similarity between them
prepositional phrase	a phrase that begins with a preposition such as *on, in, between,* or *but*

Metaphors As Prepositional Phrases

Teaching Tip

Metaphors are complex and can take many forms. This activity is one of three in which students are asked to write metaphors as different parts of speech. Do not be surprised if your students find this more challenging than you might think. However, taking the time to explore metaphors from three different angles will help your students increase their skills in writing and comprehending this type of figurative language.

Instructional Guide/Procedure

- Ask students to pair up and distribute a copy of the activity sheet to each student.

- Review the directions on the activity sheet. Spend time reviewing the examples provided, making sure that students understand the task. (10 minutes)

- Have students work in pairs to write three original metaphors. (10 minutes)

- As students are completing the activity, remind them to do the following:

  - Follow the directions in each column heading.

  - Use a thesaurus to find possible synonyms.

  - Remember that they are looking for a word or phrase that denotes something else, but can be used in place of prepositional phrases they list.

Supporting All Learners

- Students who are struggling with this activity will benefit from brainstorming a list of 8–10 prepositional phrases and then choosing three they will be able to substitute. It may also be helpful to allow these students to work in small groups instead of pairs.

- Support English language learners by allowing them to work through this activity as a group. You may want to give these students a list of prepositional phrases and help them brainstorm substitute words.

- Challenge students who are ready for more by asking them to find examples of metaphors as prepositional phrases and bring them to share with the class.

Metaphors As Prepositional Phrases

Assessment

There are various ways to assess student understanding beyond their completion of the activity sheet. Choose one or more of the following methods to evaluate their learning:

- Conduct observations while students are working.

- Ask students to write a short reflection describing their thought process as they completed this activity.

Answer Key

Answers will vary. Accept metaphors that meet the criteria described in the directions.

Name   Date

Metaphors As Prepositional Phrases

A **metaphor** is a figure of speech in which a word or phrase that denotes one thing is used in place of another to suggest a similarity between them. For example, instead of saying, "She is forgetful," the metaphor "She is an airhead," can be used to describe someone.

It is easy to confuse metaphors with similes. It helps to remember that metaphors do not use the words *like* or *as.* Writers use metaphors because they make language more interesting, encourage interpretation, and make it easier to write about complex emotions or ideas.

One way to increase your appreciation of metaphors is to experiment with writing them in different forms. In this particular activity, you will try writing a few metaphors as prepositional phrases. Here is an example.

Choose a prepositional phrase and write it in this column.	Choose a word or phrase that denotes something else, but can be used in place of the prepositional phrase in the first column.	Write your metaphor.
with care	with an eagle's eye	The teacher scrutinized my paper with an eagle's eye.
despite objections	despite the wave of protests	Despite the wave of protests, the city council upheld its decision.
but her look was unfriendly	but her eyes were ice	Fran smiled, but her eyes were ice.

(continued)

Name   Date

Metaphors As Prepositional Phrases

Now it's your turn. Complete this table to write three of your own metaphors.

Choose a prepositional phrase and write it in this column.	Choose a word that can be used in place of the prepositional phrase you wrote in the first column.	Write your metaphor.

Taking the Easy Way Out

Class Configuration

Time required:

25 minutes

Structure:

individual (activity sheet), group (discussion)

Materials:

- 1 copy of the activity sheet for each student

Learning objectives:

- Students will identify clichés used in a paragraph.

- Students will rewrite the paragraph, including the main points but without using clichés.

Standards

IRA/NCTE

6. Students apply knowledge of language structure, language conventions (e.g., spelling and punctuation), media techniques, figurative language, and genre to create, critique, and discuss print and non-print texts.

McREL

Language Arts: Standard 2. Uses the stylistic and rhetorical aspects of writing

Laying the Groundwork

Accessing students' prior knowledge will help them to develop new skills. Before starting this lesson, make sure students understand the following:

- Clichés are overused expressions.

- Good writers avoid clichés, except for those times when trite language is used to make a specific point.

- You may want to provide several examples of clichés to make sure that students clearly understand what they are.

Taking the Easy Way Out

Students should be familiar with the following vocabulary:

cliché   an expression that was once powerful or catchy, but has become so overused that it has lost its punch (Examples: "One good turn deserves another" or "Take things one step at a time")

Teaching Tip

Inexperienced writers often use clichés when they want to incorporate figurative language into their writing. They don't realize that instead of enhancing their text, they've made it boring or difficult to read. You can enhance or extend this lesson by providing additional examples of hackneyed or trite writing for students to review and revise.

Instructional Guide/Procedure

- Distribute a copy of the activity sheet to each student.

- Review the directions on the activity sheet. (5 minutes)

- Have students work independently to read, underline the clichés, and rewrite the paragraph. (15 minutes)

- At the close of the activity, ask two or three students to share their writing.

- As students are completing the activity, remind them to do the following:

  - Identify as many clichés as possible in the original paragraph before they begin writing.

  - Include all the main ideas expressed in the original paragraph.

  - Avoid use of any clichés in their revision of the paragraph.

Supporting All Learners

- Students who are struggling with this activity will benefit from working with a partner to identify the clichés before rewriting the paragraph on their own. You may also want to ask them to list the main points in the original paragraph before they begin writing.

- Support English language learners by reading the paragraph out loud and asking them what it means. Once students have identified the main points in the paragraph, point out the clichés, and ask students to brainstorm different ways to express these ideas.

- Challenge students who are ready for more by asking them to find examples of other clichés and use them to create a new paragraph that other students could rewrite for additional practice.

Taking the Easy Way Out

Assessment

There are various ways to assess student understanding beyond their completion of the activity sheet. Choose one or more of the following methods to evaluate their learning:

- Conduct observations while students are working.

- Provide another cliché-riddled paragraph and ask students to revise it.

- Provide a list of clichés and ask students to write new phrases to express the same ideas.

Answer Key

The clichés are underlined.

> The alarm rang. As Lisa groaned and shut it off, she thought "Another day, another dollar. Guess it's time to rise and shine." Being the breadwinner of the family was a tough row to hoe for any 16-year-old, but without Lisa bringing home the bacon, the family wouldn't have a penny to its name. Besides, her job now was a sweet deal and she'd be gone all in due time.

Revised paragraphs will vary. Accept responses that include the main point from the original paragraph without using clichés.

Name   Date

Taking the Easy Way Out

A **cliché** is an expression that was once powerful or catchy, but has become so overused that it has lost its punch. Familiar phrases such as "One good turn deserves another," or "Take things one step at a time," are examples. Good writers avoid clichés, except for those times when trite language is used to make a specific point.

Read the paragraph below.

> The alarm rang. As Lisa groaned and shut it off, she thought "Another day, another dollar. Guess it's time to rise and shine." Being the breadwinner of the family was a tough row to hoe for any 16-year-old, but without Lisa bringing home the bacon, the family wouldn't have a penny to its name. Besides, her job now was a sweet deal and she'd be gone all in due time.

The story of Lisa and her family has interesting possibilities, but this opening paragraph includes so many clichés that the reader will quickly stop paying attention. Underline every cliché you can find. Then rewrite the paragraph. Use figurative language that will engage, not bore, the reader.

It's Hard to Say

Class Configuration

Time required:

20 minutes

Structure:

individual (activity sheet), group (discussion)

Materials:

- 1 copy of the activity sheet for each student

Learning objectives:

- Students will write five original euphemisms.

Standards

IRA/NCTE

6. Students apply knowledge of language structure, language conventions (e.g., spelling and punctuation), media techniques, figurative language, and genre to create, critique, and discuss print and non-print texts.

McREL

Language Arts: Standard 2. Uses the stylistic and rhetorical aspects of writing

Laying the Groundwork

Accessing students' prior knowledge will help them to develop new skills. Before starting this lesson, make sure students understand that people often use euphemisms when they are uncomfortable with speaking plainly.

Students should be familiar with the following vocabulary:

euphemism   use of an inoffensive word or phrase to express something that people often find uncomfortable or embarrassing to say

It's Hard to Say

Teaching Tip

This activity can be extended or enhanced by encouraging students to write or collect additional examples of euphemisms for the meanings provided, and then using these euphemisms to write a dialogue between two characters who do not want to speak frankly with one another.

Instructional Guide/Procedure

- Distribute a copy of the activity sheet to each student.

- Review the directions on the activity sheet. Spend time reviewing the examples provided, making sure that students understand the task. (5 minutes)

- Have students complete the activity. (10 minutes)

- Ask a few volunteers to share one of the euphemisms they wrote. (5 minutes)

- As students are completing the activity, remind them to do the following:

  - Brainstorm words they can use to create each euphemism.

  - Think of kind or neutral ways to express the meaning.

  - Keep familiar euphemisms in mind.

Supporting All Learners

- Students who are struggling with this activity will benefit from working through one example with assistance before tackling the activity independently. Discussing typical attributes of the kind of person or situation referred to in the meaning will also be helpful.

- Support English language learners by leading them through this activity as a group. You may also want to supply a sample euphemism for each meaning, and then help the students write original euphemisms.

- Challenge students who are ready for more by asking them to find at least three existing euphemisms for each meaning in the activity.

It's Hard to Say

Assessment

There are various ways to assess student understanding beyond their completion of the activity sheet. Choose one or more of the following methods to evaluate their learning:

- Conduct observations while students are working.

- Ask students to use each original euphemism in a sentence.

- Have students find and bring to class two to three examples of euphemisms they hear or read.

Answer Key

Responses will vary. Accept answers that are original and meet the definition of euphemism.

Name _____   Date _____

It's Hard to Say

A **euphemism** is the use of an inoffensive word or phrase to express something that people often find uncomfortable or embarrassing to say. Familiar euphemisms include the following:

Meaning	Euphemism
crime suspect	person of interest
obese	full-figured
lazy	motivationally challenged
not very smart	six bricks short of a full load

Use the chart below to write an original euphemism for each meaning provided.

Meaning	Euphemism
old person	
liar	
rich	
stolen goods	
war	

Half Full or Half Empty?

Class Configuration

Time required:

20 minutes

Structure:

individual (activity sheet), group (discussion)

Materials:

- 1 copy of the activity sheet for each student

Learning objectives:

- Students will use litotes to rewrite five sentences so they have the same meaning using negative statements.

Standards

IRA/NCTE

6. Students apply knowledge of language structure, language conventions (e.g., spelling and punctuation), media techniques, figurative language, and genre to create, critique, and discuss print and non-print texts.

McREL

Language Arts: Standard 2. Uses the stylistic and rhetorical aspects of writing

Laying the Groundwork

Accessing students' prior knowledge will help them to develop new skills. Before starting this lesson, make sure students understand the following:

- People sometimes speak negatively to make a positive point. This is called *litotes*.

- Litotes are used to draw readers' and listeners' attention to something specific.

Students should be familiar with the following vocabulary:

litotes	a figure of speech in which the speaker emphasizes the magnitude of a statement by denying its opposite (Example: "That boy's not dumb," actually means, "That boy is intelligent.")
double negative	use of two negative words to make a strong positive statement

Half Full or Half Empty?

Teaching Tip

This activity can be extended or enhanced by encouraging students to listen for examples of litotes in conversations and record them in journal entries.

Instructional Guide/Procedure

- Distribute a copy of the activity sheet to each student.

- Review the directions on the activity sheet. Spend time reviewing the examples provided, making sure that students understand the task. (5 minutes)

- Have students rewrite the sentences using litotes. (10 minutes)

- Ask a few volunteers to share some of the sentences they rewrote. (5 minutes)

- As students are completing the activity, remind them to do the following:

  - Read each sentence carefully.

  - Identify the positive words and determine how they could be expressed as double negatives.

Supporting All Learners

- Students who are struggling with this activity will benefit from working through one or more examples with assistance before finishing the activity with a partner.

- Support English language learners by leading them through this activity as a group.

- Challenge students who are ready for more by asking them to write a conversation using litotes.

Assessment

There are various ways to assess student understanding beyond their completion of the activity sheet. Choose one or more of the following methods to evaluate their learning:

- Conduct observations while students are working.

- Ask students to write a reflection about the thought process they used while rewriting the sentences using litotes.

Adolescent Literacy: Figurative Language

Half Full or Half Empty?

Answer Key

Responses may vary slightly, but should be similar to the following:

Sentences	Litotes
I'd like to get a perfect score on the next test.	I'd like to not fail the next test.
We've experienced four tornadoes this spring.	Tornadoes are not unusual around here this spring.
That new pair of shoes costs $150.	Those shoes don't come cheap.
That blogger says what he means.	That blogger isn't shy.
My grandmother sets a good example for us all.	My grandmother always does the right thing.

Name   Date

Half Full or Half Empty?

Litotes are a figure of speech in which the speaker emphasizes the magnitude of a statement by denying its opposite. For example, "That boy's not dumb," actually means, "That boy is intelligent." People often use litotes because they want to draw readers' or listeners' attention to something specific.

Read the sentences in the table below. Rewrite the sentences using litotes to convey the same meaning using negative statements.

Sentences	Litotes
I'd like to get a perfect score on the next test.	
We've experienced four tornadoes this spring.	
That new pair of shoes costs $150.	
That blogger says what he means.	
My grandmother sets a good example for us all.	

extending and enhancing learning

Let's stay in touch!

Thank you for purchasing these Walch Education materials. Now, we'd like to support you in your role as an educator. **Register now** and we'll provide you with updates on related publications, online resources, and more. You can register online at www.walch.com/newsletter, or fill out this form and fax or mail it to us.

Name _____ Date _____

School name _____

School address_____

City _____ State _____ Zip _____

Phone number (home) _____ (school) _____

E-mail _____

Grade level(s) taught _____ Subject area(s) _____

Where did you purchase this publication? _____

When do you primarily purchase supplemental materials? _____

What moneys were used to purchase this publication?

[   ] School supplemental budget

[   ] Federal/state funding

[   ] Personal

[   ] Please sign me up for Walch Education's free quarterly e-newsletter, *Education Connection.*

[   ] Please notify me regarding free *Teachable Moments* downloads.

[   ] Yes, you may use my comments in upcoming communications.

COMMENTS _____

_____

_____

_____

Please FAX this completed form to 888-991-5755, or mail it to:

Customer Service, Walch Education, 40 Walch Drive, Portland, ME 04103

www.walch.com